TAPAS

Simple and Delicious
TAPAS

Richard Tapper

APPLE

Contents

Introducing Tapas

To the average Spaniard, the local tapas bar provides the three things held dearest—good food, good wine and the opportunity to offer an opinion in convivial conversation. Much of Spain's social and business conversation is held in cafés and bars, and no one would dream of a drink without *algo para picar*—something to nibble at; in other words, tapas.

The word tapa literally means "lid," and the origin of the tapas custom most probably lies in the placing of a small plate or lid over a glass of wine when served. It is also said that a centuries-old decree insisted all bars and roadhouses serve food as an accompaniment to wine, in an attempt to ensure at least a modicum of sobriety among the nation's coach drivers.

Whatever its origins may have been, the daily gathering before lunch or dinner for the ritual partaking of tapas, as both an appetizer and an adjunct to conversation, is now an integral part of the Spanish way of life. Tapas have evolved into an almost separate style of cuisine.

Tapas are a tradition long peculiar to Spain, but the last two decades have seen their growing popularity in the United States, particularly New York and California, and internationally, where the proliferation of tapas bars is a testament to the public's willingness to embrace the nation known for a more sensible social style of drinking. Tapas, while remaining quintessentially Spanish, lend themselves easily to adaptation.

Many recipes in this book are authentically Spanish. You'll also find exciting variations. When serving tapas, try presenting them in Spanish crockery. You might have Spanish classical guitar music playing in the background to help create the slightly eccentric conviviality of an authentic Spanish tapas bar.

Buen provecho!

Step-by-step Guide

Empanada pastry

The filled pastries known as empanadas come in many varieties. Not only are they common in Spain but they can also be found throughout Central and South America. The secret of getting empanadas right is having the filling mixture at the right consistency and the pastry at the right temperature.

A good filling should be reasonably thick, with no oil or liquids exuding from it (which would make it difficult to join the pastry edges together). The filling should be cold so that it doesn't soften the dough. It's best to keep the pastry circles in the refrigerator, filling only four or five at a time.

Although homemade pastry produces an admirably better result, already-prepared empanada pastry is available in Spanish and South American delicatessens. You can also use a commercial puff or short pastry; the type that comes in rolled sheets is already the approximate thickness required for empanadas. After you have cut out the circles, let them rest in the refrigerator for at least 30 minutes and take out just a few at a time as described below.

Makes enough for 60 empanadas

9 cups (2¼ lb/1 kg) all-purpose (plain) flour

approximately 2 cups (16 fl oz/500 ml) cold water

generous pinch of salt

1 lb (500 g) butter, at room temperature

1. Pile flour on a pastry board and make a well in center. Gradually mix in enough water to make a smooth, workable dough, adding salt at some point during this process. Knead dough for at least 7–8 minutes, continually turning and folding it back onto itself. Wrap dough in plastic wrap and let rest in refrigerator for at least 30 minutes.

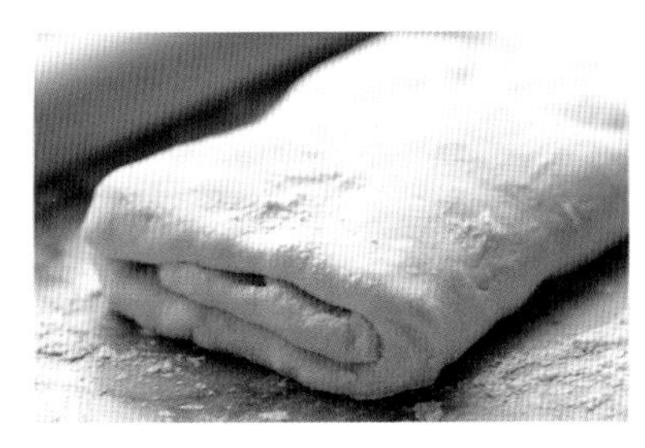

2. On a floured board, roll out dough into a large, thin sheet. Spread butter (which should be room-temperature soft, but not melting) evenly over dough. Fold edges into center at least 4 times. Wrap and return dough to refrigerator for 30 minutes.

3. Again roll out dough on floured board and fold over at least 8 times. Return to refrigerator for another 30 minutes, then roll dough to 1⁄16 inch (2 mm) thick and cut into 4-inch (10-cm) circles. Press scraps together and roll into additional circles. Lightly flour circles and return to refrigerator for 30 minutes. Bring them out 4 or 5 at a time to fill.

4. Place 1–2 teaspoons filling in center of each circle. Fold in half and pinch edge between your thumb and forefinger, turning edge inward to ensure that filling remains enclosed.

Marinated olives

Aceitunas aliñadas

The secret of marinating your own olives is to leave them marinating as long as possible—a minimum of three weeks and a maximum of six months.

Green olives

8 oz (250 g) canned or bulk green olives, pits intact
12 large cloves garlic, crushed
1 tablespoon chopped fennel bulb
olive oil as needed

Drain off any liquid from olives and lightly crush olives. Put in a sealable glass jar with the garlic and fennel. Pour in olive oil to cover. Cover and store in refrigerator, turning occasionally. Serve at room temperature.

Black olives

8 oz (250 g) black olives, pits intact
2–12 cloves garlic, crushed
1–2 dried red chili peppers
red wine vinegar as needed
dash of lemon juice

Drain off any liquid from olives and lightly crush olives. Put in a sealable glass jar with garlic to taste and chilies. Pour in red wine vinegar to cover and add lemon juice. Cover and store at room temperature for at least 3 weeks.

Marinated olives

Piquant olives

8 oz (250 g) large green olives
8 green chili peppers
white wine vinegar as needed
dash of lemon juice

Remove pits from olives and place in a sealable jar with chili peppers. Pour in white wine vinegar to cover and add lemon juice. Store at room temperature for at least 3 weeks. These olives are a favorite in Spanish tapas bars and are great appetizers with predinner drinks.

Roasted peppers

Pimientos asados

Roasted peppers (capsicums) are used on their own, as an integral part of many other dishes and as a garnish. If served whole as tapas, it is best to use small peppers. When the peppers are used as an ingredient or garnish, they are invariably cut into thin strips or are finely diced. They also make an excellent addition to chicken or seafood salads. For a stand-alone dish, you will need 6 red bell peppers. Serves 6

1. Brush peppers with olive oil and bake in a 350–400°F (180–200°C/ Gas 4–6) oven for about 30 minutes. Alternatively, roast on a charcoal or stove-top grill pan for a shorter time.

2. The peppers are cooked as soon as they collapse and portions of the skin are blackened.

3. Place peppers into a plastic bag or wrap in aluminum foil. Seal and stand for 10 minutes. Remove, peel and seed peppers.

4. Toss with a dressing of olive oil, a little lemon juice and salt and pepper. If you wish, add a bit of anchovy, chopped onion and parsley.

Vegetables

Stuffed artichokes

Alcachofas rellenas

Serves 8

8 artichokes
olive oil as needed
1/2 cup (3 oz/100 g) minced onion
8 oz (250 g) ground (minced) lean pork
3 oz (90 g) ground (minced) ham
1/2 cup (2 oz/60 g) breadcrumbs
2 tablespoons chopped fresh parsley
salt and freshly ground pepper
Zesty tomato sauce (see page 59)

Trim top ¾–1¼ inch (2–3 cm) from artichokes. Bring a pot of salted water to a boil, add artichokes and cook until tender (do not overcook).

In a frying pan over medium heat, warm about 1 tablespoon olive oil. Add onion, pork and ham and fry until pork is barely cooked. Remove from heat and drain off any excess fat. Add breadcrumbs, parsley, salt and pepper, and mix well.

Pull leaves of each artichoke outward to expose prickly choke. Remove choke, being sure to leave heart intact. Fill each artichoke with stuffing.

Preheat oven to 350°F (180°C/Gas 4). Cut stem from each artichoke so artichoke will stand upright. Arrange artichokes in a baking pan. Sprinkle with a little olive oil and bake for 20 minutes. Serve hot with Zesty tomato sauce.

Stuffed eggplant

Berenjenas rellenas

Serves 8

1 tablespoon olive oil
2 large onions, finely chopped
4 cloves garlic, finely chopped
1 1/2 teaspoons peeled and finely chopped fresh ginger
1 lb (500 g) fresh or canned tomatoes
chopped basil, to taste
chopped cilantro (coriander), to taste
4 small/medium eggplants (aubergines)
about 1/4 cup (2 fl oz/60 ml) olive oil
1 large onion, finely chopped
6 cloves garlic, finely chopped
1 celery stalk, finely chopped
1 red bell pepper (capsicum), seeded and finely chopped
1 1/2 tablespoons self-rising flour
1 cup (4 oz/125 g) fresh breadcrumbs
2 egg whites, beaten
salt and freshly ground pepper
2 tablespoons grated Parmesan cheese
basil sprigs, for garnish

To make herbed tomato sauce: In a frying pan over medium heat, warm olive oil. Add onions, garlic and ginger and fry for 3 minutes. Add tomatoes and cook for 10 minutes. Puree in a food processor, then add basil and cilantro. Measure 1 cup (8 fl oz/250 ml) sauce; set aside remainder.

Preheat oven to 475°F (240°C/Gas 9). Cut eggplants in half lengthwise and deeply score flesh in a crisscross pattern, being careful not to cut skin. Use 2 tablespoons of oil to coat flesh, then place slices on a baking sheet and bake until almost cooked through, 8–10 minutes. Scoop out flesh, leaving a shell about 3/8 inch (1 cm) thick. Puree flesh and set aside.

In a frying pan over medium heat, warm 1 tablespoon of olive oil. Add onion and garlic and fry for 3 minutes. Add celery and bell pepper and cook for 3 minutes. Add reserved tomato sauce and eggplant puree and cook for 5 minutes. Remove from heat and stir in flour and breadcrumbs. Let cool for 10 minutes, then fold in egg whites. Season with salt and pepper.

Stuff eggplant shells with tomato mixture and place in an oiled baking dish. Cover half of each stuffed eggplant with Parmesan cheese. Bake until browned, 10–15 minutes. Spoon remaining sauce over other half of each eggplant and garnish with basil sprigs.

Fried eggplant with Parmesan

Berenjenas con queso

Serves 8

2 medium eggplants (aubergines)
2 eggs
4 cloves garlic, minced
1/4 cup (2 fl oz/60 ml) water
1 cup (8 fl oz/250 ml) olive oil
flour as needed
7 oz (220 g) Parmesan cheese, finely grated

Cut eggplants into batons 2 inches by 1/2 inch (5 cm by 12 mm). In a bowl, mix eggs, garlic and water.

In a frying pan over medium-high heat, warm olive oil. Dredge eggplant slices in flour, dip in egg mixture and then dip in cheese, making sure both sides are coated. Fry until golden brown, about 2 minutes on each side. Drain on paper towels. Serve immediately.

Potatoes in spicy sauce

Patatas bravas

Serves 8

5 tablespoons olive oil
8 large potatoes, peeled and cut into 1½-inch (4-cm) cubes
1 large onion, finely chopped
3 cloves garlic, finely chopped
2 tablespoons finely chopped parsley
½ cup (4 fl oz/125 ml) dry white wine
3 fresh chili peppers, seeded and chopped,
or 1 tablespoon Chili sauce (see page 58)
2 cups (16 fl oz/500 ml) canned plum (Roma) tomatoes, pureed
salt to taste
chorizo or chopped bacon to taste (optional)

Preheat oven to 475°F (240°C/Gas 9). Heat 4 tablespoons of olive oil in a frying pan over high heat until smoking. Add potato and brown thoroughly. Transfer potatoes and oil to a baking dish and bake until potatoes are crisp, about 15 minutes.

Meanwhile, heat the remaining 1 tablespoon oil in a frying pan over medium heat and sauté onion and garlic for 3 minutes. Add remaining ingredients and simmer sauce for 10–12 minutes. Drain potatoes and place in a serving bowl or individual dishes. Pour sauce over potatoes and toss—there should be just enough sauce to coat. Serve at once.

Potato salad

Ensaladilla

Serves 8

6 potatoes, boiled, peeled and diced
1/2 cup (2 oz/60 g) diced cooked carrot
1/2 cup (2 oz/60 g) cooked green peas
1 cup (8 fl oz/250 ml) Garlic mayonnaise (see page 59)
salt and freshly ground pepper
1 red and 1 green bell pepper (capsicum), roasted, peeled and seeded (see page 12), then cut into strips
parsley sprigs, for garnish

In a bowl, mix potatoes, carrot, peas, mayonnaise and salt and pepper to taste. Mound on a platter, top with pepper strips and garnish with parsley.

The flavor will improve if the salad is left standing for an hour at room temperature.

HINT This mayonnaise-and-potato salad, found in every tapas bar in Spain, is invariably one of the first dishes to be presented each day. It begins as a highly decorated mound of salad on a large platter and diminishes as the day progresses.

Stuffed mushrooms

Champiñones rellenos

Serves 8

1/4 cup (2 fl oz/60 ml) olive oil
1 1/2 teaspoons finely chopped garlic
32 button mushrooms, about 2 inches (5 cm) in diameter, stems removed
1 tablespoon finely chopped onion
1/4 cup (1 oz/30 g) minced tocino or bacon
1 tablespoon finely chopped parsley
2 eggs, lightly beaten
2 tablespoons fresh breadcrumbs
2 tablespoons freshly grated Parmesan cheese

Heat olive oil in a frying pan large enough to hold mushrooms. Add garlic, then mushrooms, tops down, and sauté gently until browned but not cooked through, about 2 minutes. Remove mushrooms. Add onion and tocino to pan and sauté for 2–3 minutes. Pour off any excess liquid. Add parsley, remove from heat and let cool. Add eggs and breadcrumbs and mix well. Stuff mushroom caps with tocino mixture and top each with Parmesan cheese. Broil (grill) or bake in an oven preheated to 450°F (230°C/Gas 9) until cheese is browned and mushrooms are cooked through. Serve at once.

Mushrooms in garlic and parsley

Champiñones al ajillo

Serves 8

1/4 cup (2 fl oz/60 ml) olive oil
6 cloves garlic, finely chopped
1 lb (500 g) mushrooms
2 tablespoons chopped parsley
1 tablespoon flour
1 cup (8 fl oz/250 ml) water
salt and freshly ground pepper
juice of 1/2 lemon

In a frying pan over medium heat, warm oil. Add garlic and fry for 1–2 minutes, making sure garlic doesn't burn. Add mushrooms and parsley and cook until mushrooms begin to exude liquid.

Add flour and stir constantly until liquid becomes a paste, then stir in water, salt, pepper and lemon juice. Simmer for 10 minutes, adding a little more water if sauce is too thick. Serve hot.

Mushrooms with bacon

Champiñones con tocino

Serves 6

1 tablespoon olive oil
4 oz (125 g) diced tocino or bacon
2 cloves garlic, finely chopped
1 lb (500 g) button mushrooms
1/2 cup (4 fl oz/125 ml) dry white wine
salt
2 teaspoons freshly ground pepper
1 tablespoon chopped parsley

In a frying pan over high heat, warm olive oil. Add tocino and fry for 3 minutes. Add garlic and mushrooms and stir well. Add wine, salt, pepper and parsley and cook over high heat until most of wine has evaporated and mushrooms are cooked, 3–4 minutes. Serve hot.

Batter-fried vegetables

Verduras fritas

Serves 15–20

1 cup (8 fl oz/250 ml) cold water
1 cup (4 oz/125 g) all-purpose (plain) flour
1/2 cup (2 oz/60 g) cornstarch (cornflour)
pinch of salt
dash of lemon juice
1 egg yolk
oil, for frying
1 eggplant (aubergine), thinly sliced crosswise
2 large onions, sliced into rings
1/2 cauliflower, cut into small florets, blanched for 3–4 minutes and drained
2 zucchini (courgettes), cut into thin strips 2 inches (5 cm) long
1 red or green bell pepper (capsicum), cut into strips 2 inches x 3/8 inch (5 cm x 1 cm)
seasoned flour, for dredging
lemon wedges, for serving
Garlic mayonnaise (see page 59)

In a bowl, whisk cold water with flour and cornstarch until completely smooth. (When you dip a finger into batter, it should run off, leaving just a thin coating on your finger.) Whisk in salt, lemon juice and egg yolk. Refrigerate batter for about 15 minutes. Pour oil in a frying pan to a depth of 3 inches (7.5 cm) and heat to 350°F (180°C) on a deep-frying thermometer. Working in batches, dredge vegetables in seasoned flour, shaking off excess, then dip into batter. Deep-fry vegetables until golden brown. Drain on paper towels. Serve immediately with lemon wedges and Garlic mayonnaise.

NOTE This popular dish could be compared with tempura. (Tempura did, in fact, originate on the Iberian Peninsula, having been introduced to Japan by the Portuguese several hundred years ago.) In Spain, the vegetables are served with lemon wedges or garlic mayonnaise.

Stuffed red peppers

Pimientos rellenos

Serves 6–8

6–8 small red bell peppers (capsicums)
2 tablespoons olive oil, plus extra for brushing
1/2 cup (2 oz/60 g) chopped onion
2 cloves garlic, finely chopped
3–5 oz (90–150 g) canned tomatoes, finely chopped
2 red chili peppers, seeded and chopped
12 mussels, cooked and diced
1 can (8 oz/250 g) whole clams, drained
1 tablespoon chopped parsley
salt and freshly ground pepper
1/2 cup (2 oz/60 g) cooked white rice

Preheat oven to 400°F (200°C/Gas 6). Brush bell peppers with a little olive oil, place on a baking sheet and roast for 15 minutes. Cut around stem of each pepper, pull it out and reserve. Remove seeds.

Heat 2 tablespoons olive oil in a frying pan over medium heat and sauté onion and garlic until transparent. Add tomatoes and chilies and cook until reduced to a smooth sauce. Add mussels, clams, parsley, and salt and pepper to taste. Remove from heat and add rice.

Preheat oven to 375°F (190°C/Gas 5). Stuff peppers with rice mixture. Do not overfill as rice needs room to expand. Replace stems. Arrange peppers in a baking dish and brush with a little olive oil. Bake until heated through, 10–15 minutes. Serve hot.

Pastries

Spinach pastries

Empanadas de espinacas

Serves 8–10

1 tablespoon olive oil
2 cloves garlic, finely chopped
2 tablespoons finely diced chorizo or ham (optional)
1 large bunch spinach, stemmed, washed and chopped
1 red bell pepper (capsicum), roasted, peeled and seeded (see page 12), then cut into strips
salt and freshly ground pepper
Empanada pastry (see page 8)
1 egg beaten with 2 teaspoons water

Heat oil in a frying pan over medium heat. Add garlic and chorizo and fry for 1 minute. Add spinach and toss until wilted. Add bell pepper strips and remove from heat. Let cool.

Squeeze out any liquid from spinach mixture. Season with salt and pepper. Put 2 teaspoons spinach mixture in center of each pastry circle, remembering to take circles from refrigerator only 4 or 5 at a time. Fold circles over filling and crimp edges. Refrigerate for at least 15 minutes.

Preheat oven to 475°F (240°C/Gas 9). Arrange empanadas at least ¾ inch (2 cm) apart on a greased baking sheet. Brush with egg wash. Bake until golden brown, 5–6 minutes. Serve immediately.

Fish pastries

Empanadas de pescado

Serves 8–10

2 tablespoons olive oil
1/2 cup (2 oz/60 g) finely chopped onion
2 cloves garlic, finely chopped
1 large tomato, chopped
1 red chili pepper, seeded and chopped
salt and freshly ground pepper
1 tablespoon tomato paste diluted with a little water
1 tablespoon chopped parsley
8 oz (250 g) cooked and boned firm-fleshed fish such as tuna or cod
1 hard-boiled egg, chopped
1 red bell pepper (capsicum), roasted, peeled and seeded (see page 12), then diced
empanada pastry (see page 8)
1 egg beaten with 2 teaspoons water

Heat oil in a frying pan over medium heat. Add onion and garlic and fry until transparent. Add tomato, chili and salt and pepper to taste and cook until somewhat thickened. Add diluted tomato paste and parsley and cook for 3–4 minutes. Remove from heat and let cool. Mix in fish, egg and bell pepper.

Preheat oven to 475°F (240°C/Gas 9). Put 2 teaspoons fish mixture in center of each pastry circle, remembering to take only 4 or 5 circles from refrigerator at a time. Fold circle over filling and crimp edges. Refrigerate for at least 15 minutes.

Arrange empanadas at least 3/4 inch (2 cm) apart on a greased baking sheet. Brush with egg wash. Bake until golden brown, 5–6 minutes. Serve immediately.

Chorizo and olive empanadas

Empanadas de chorizo y aceitunas

Serves 6–8

2 oz (60 g) chorizo, finely chopped
1 oz (30 g) pimiento-stuffed green olives, finely chopped
1 tablespoon finely chopped red bell pepper (capsicum)
24 Empanada pastry circles (see page 8)
1 egg beaten with 2 teaspoons water

In a bowl, mix chorizo, olives and bell pepper. Put 1–2 teaspoons chorizo mixture in center of each pastry circle, remembering to take only 4 or 5 circles from refrigerator at a time. Fold circle over filling and crimp edges. Refrigerate at least 15 minutes.

Preheat oven to 475°F (240°C/Gas 9). Arrange empanadas at least ¾ inch (2 cm) apart on a lightly greased baking sheet. Brush with egg wash. Bake until golden brown and pastry is cooked through, about 5 minutes. Serve immediately.

Spicy shrimp and scallop empanadas

Empanadas de mariscos picantes

Serves 8–10

2 tablespoons butter
8 oz (250 g) jumbo shrimp (king prawns), peeled and chopped
7 oz (220 g) scallops, chopped
1 onion, finely chopped
2 cloves garlic, finely chopped
1 1/2 teaspoons peeled and finely chopped fresh ginger
1 tablespoon hot Madras curry powder
1 tablespoon flour
1/2 cup (4 fl oz/125 ml) unsweetened thin coconut cream or coconut milk
1 tablespoon chopped fresh cilantro (coriander)
salt (optional)
1 1/2 teaspoons Chili sauce (see page 58), or to taste
Empanada pastry (see page 8)
1 egg beaten with 2 teaspoons water

In a frying pan over medium heat, melt 1 tablespoon of butter. Add chopped shrimp and scallops and gently sauté until shrimp change color (they should not be cooked through). Place in a colander, refresh under cold running water and set aside.

In a frying pan, melt remaining 1 tablespoon butter and sauté onion, garlic and ginger for about 3 minutes. Add curry powder and flour and cook, stirring constantly, to make a roux, about 3 minutes. Add coconut cream, cilantro, salt (if using) and Chili sauce and cook for 3–4 minutes, stirring to make sure mixture is smooth. Add shrimp and scallops and immediately remove from heat. Let mixture cool.

Preheat oven to 475°F (240°C/Gas 9). Put 2 teaspoons seafood mixture in center of each pastry circle, remembering to take only 4 or 5 circles from refrigerator at a time. Fold circle over filling and crimp edges. Refrigerate for at least 15 minutes. Arrange empanadas at least 3/4 inch (2 cm) apart on a greased baking sheet. Brush with egg wash. Bake until golden brown, 5–6 minutes. Serve immediately.

Eggs

Andalusian baked eggs

Huevos a la flamenca

Serves 6

2 tablespoons olive oil
1 onion, finely chopped
2 cloves garlic, finely chopped
1 lb (500 g) canned whole peeled plum (Roma) tomatoes, coarsely chopped
1 cup (6 oz/180 g) diced serrano ham or proscuitto
12 eggs
2 chorizo sausages, cut in rounds 3/8 inch (1 cm) thick
24 pencil-thin asparagus spears, blanched
1 red bell pepper (capsicum), roasted, peeled and seeded (see page 12), then cut into strips
1 tablespoon finely chopped parsley
freshly ground pepper

Heat oil in a frying pan over medium heat. Add onion and garlic and fry for 3 minutes. Add tomatoes and cook for 10 minutes. In a separate pan over medium heat, cook ham and chorizo for 3 minutes.

Preheat oven to 400°F (200°C/Gas 6). Divide tomato mixture among 6 individual ramekins. Break 2 eggs into each ramekin and then arrange ham, chorizo, asparagus spears and bell pepper strips around them. Sprinkle with parsley and season with pepper. Bake until egg whites are cooked but yolks are still runny, about 10 minutes. Serve at once.

HINTS As the name suggests, this dish has its origins in Andalusia, the southern province of Spain, which is home to a large proportion of the country's gypsy population. You can vary this dish by adding a tablespoon of Chili sauce (see page 58) to the tomato mixture. You can also give it a sprinkling of Parmesan cheese, but don't overdo it.

Spicy hard-boiled eggs

Huevos duros picantes

Serves 8

2 tablespoons olive oil
2 cloves garlic, finely chopped
2 teaspoons peeled and finely chopped fresh ginger
1 onion, finely sliced
1 teaspoon ground cumin
1 teaspoon ground coriander
1 teaspoon ground turmeric
1 tablespoon seeded and chopped red chili pepper
1½ cups (12 fl oz/375 ml) unsweetened thin coconut cream or coconut milk
8 hard-boiled eggs
cilantro (coriander) sprigs for garnish

In a large frying pan, warm oil over medium heat. Fry garlic, ginger and onion until onion is transparent. Add ground spices and chili and cook for another 2 minutes, stirring constantly. Remove from heat and allow to cool.

Blend onion-spice mixture in a food processor with coconut cream. Return mixture to pan and bring to a boil. Add eggs, reduce heat to low and simmer for 30 minutes, stirring occasionally. Serve garnished with cilantro sprigs.

Salmon-stuffed eggs

Huevos duros rellenos

Serves 6

6 hard-boiled eggs
1 can (3–5 oz/90–150 g) red salmon, drained
6 green olives, pitted and finely chopped
2 tablespoons mayonnaise
1 teaspoon paprika
1 1/2 teaspoons chopped parsley
2 teaspoons lemon juice
salt and freshly ground pepper
1 slice smoked salmon, cut into strips
1 green bell pepper (capsicum), seeded and cut into thin strips

Halve eggs lengthwise. Remove yolks and reserve 4 for another use. Place remaining 2 yolks in a bowl and add remaining ingredients except smoked salmon and bell pepper. Blend well.

Transfer yolk mixture to a pastry (icing) bag and fill egg whites with mixture. Arrange smoked salmon and bell pepper strips on top.

Zucchini omelette

Tortilla de calabacines

Serves 12

10–13 oz (300–400 g) zucchini (courgettes), cut into slices about 3/8 inch (1 cm) thick
12 eggs
salt and freshly ground pepper
2 tablespoons olive oil
1/2 cup (2 oz/60 g) finely chopped onion
1 clove garlic, finely chopped

In a covered steamer set over boiling water, steam zucchini until tender but not soggy, about 3 minutes. Alternatively, cook in 3/4 inch (2 cm) boiling water for 3 minutes. Drain.

In a large bowl, beat eggs with salt and pepper to taste. Heat 1 tablespoon of oil in a frying pan about 8 inches (20 cm) wide and with sloping sides 2 inches (5 cm) deep over medium heat. Add onion and garlic and sauté 2–3 minutes. Drain and add to eggs along with zucchini.

In the same pan, heat remaining 1 tablespoon oil until smoking. Pour in egg mixture and stir away from pan bottom 5 or 6 times. Cook until omelette is set two-thirds of the way through, place a large plate over pan and invert omelette onto it. Slide omelette back into pan, uncooked side down, and cook until set throughout. Divide into 12 equal portions and serve.

Spicy shrimp omelette

Tortilla de gambas picantes

Serves 8

3 tablespoons olive oil, plus extra as needed
2 large potatoes, peeled and thinly sliced
1 large onion, thinly sliced
15 eggs
1 teaspoon salt
4 red chili peppers, seeded and chopped, or 1 tablespoon chili sauce **(see page 106)**
2 cups (12 oz/375 g) peeled, deveined and chopped jumbo shrimp (king prawns)

Heat 2 tablespoons of olive oil in a pan about 6–8 inches (15–20 cm) wide and with sloping sides about 2 inches (5 cm) deep over medium heat. When oil begins to smoke, spread half of potatoes evenly in pan, top with onion and then add remaining potatoes. Turn mixture frequently until potatoes are cooked; take care not to burn them. Remove from heat.

Beat eggs with salt in a bowl large enough to hold all ingredients. Stir in chilies, shrimp and potato mixture. Wipe pan clean, add remaining 1 tablespoon oil and heat until smoking. Add egg mixture and stir away from pan bottom 5 or 6 times. When omelette is half cooked, reduce heat, shake pan and run a spatula around side to prevent omelette from sticking. When omelette is almost cooked, place a large place over pan and invert onto it.

Return pan to high heat, making sure nothing is sticking to it, and add more oil if needed. Slide omelette back into pan, uncooked side down. Reduce heat and cook until omelette is set throughout. Invert onto a plate and let stand for a few minutes before cutting into wedges. Serve warm or, as is more typical in Spain, at room temperature.

Meat and poultry

Meatballs

Albóndigas

Serves 12

1 lb (500 g) ground (minced) pork or beef
1/2 cup (2 oz/60 g) finely chopped onion
4 cloves garlic, finely chopped
1 tablespoon chopped parsley
1/2 cup (2 oz/60 g) fine breadcrumbs
3 eggs
1 red chili pepper, minced, or a dash of Chili sauce (see page 58)
freshly ground pepper
salt
flour, for coating
oil, for frying

In a bowl, combine all ingredients except flour and oil, mixing thoroughly. Let stand for 30 minutes to allow flavors to blend.

In a frying pan, heat enough oil to cover meatballs; oil is ready when it reaches 350°F (180°C) on a deep-frying thermometer. Roll meatballs in flour. Deep-fry, turning once, until cooked through. Drain on paper towels and serve immediately.

NOTE In Spain one would usually prepare this dish using ground (minced) pork, but beef is a good alternative. The following recipe will produce about 40–50 meatballs if you make them about 1 inch (2.5 cm) in diameter. When served as tapas, meatballs are traditionally presented with Garlic mayonnaise (see page 59) as a dip or are reheated in a rich tomato sauce such as Simple tomato sauce (see page 59).

Moorish-style kabobs

Pinchos morunos

Serves 8

½ cup (4 fl oz/125 ml) olive oil

1 teaspoon chopped fresh thyme

1 teaspoon chili powder

1 teaspoon paprika

2 teaspoons ground cumin

1 teaspoon freshly ground pepper

1 teaspoon salt

1½ teaspoons chopped parsley

1–1½ lb (500–750 g) lean pork, cut into ¾-inch (2-cm) cubes

Combine all ingredients except pork in a large glass or ceramic bowl. Add pork and stir to coat well. Cover and refrigerate overnight. Start a fire in a charcoal grill. Drain pork, reserving marinade.

Thread pork cubes on skewers. In a small pan, bring marinade to a boil. Remove from heat, then set aside. When coals are hot, cook pork to desired doneness, basting frequently with marinade. Serve at once.

Sangría

Red wine punch

This sweet red wine punch is a Spanish original that complements tapas food. It is perfect for a warm afternoon as it is cooling and refreshing. Be aware though, it's more alcoholic than its mild taste suggests! This recipe makes 6 cups.

4 cups (32 fl oz/1 L) light-bodied red wine, well chilled

¾ cup (6 fl oz/180 ml) brandy

2 cups (16 fl oz/500 ml) soda water

½ cup (4 oz/120 g) superfine (caster) sugar

1 orange, sliced

6–8 strawberries, halved

Mix wine, brandy and sugar, stirring to dissolve sugar. Chill well. Just before serving, add the soda water and fruit.

Chicken legs

Piernas de pollo

Serves 8

16 chicken legs, skin removed
flour, for dredging
olive oil, for frying
1 onion, finely chopped
1 tablespoon chopped garlic
1 lb (500 g) canned whole peeled plum (Roma) tomatoes
1 cup (8 fl oz/250 ml) chicken stock
salt and freshly ground pepper

Preheat oven to 300°F (150°C/Gas 2). Dredge chicken legs in flour. In a frying pan over medium heat, warm oil. Fry chicken, turning as needed, until evenly browned. Remove from pan. Pour off excess oil. Return pan to medium heat and sauté onion and garlic until onion is transparent. Add tomatoes and cook for 15 minutes. Remove from heat and puree in a blender or food processor with chicken stock. Season with salt and pepper.

Arrange chicken legs in a baking dish and cover with tomato sauce. Cover with aluminum foil and bake for 1 hour. Remove foil, turn chicken in sauce, pour off any excess liquid and bake until chicken is tender, about 30 minutes. Serve immediately.

Seafood

Deep-fried squid

Calamares a la romana

Serves 8

oil, for frying

2 lb (1 kg) fresh squid (calamari), cleaned (see page 61)

flour, for dredging

4 eggs mixed with 2 tablespoons water

breadcrumbs, for coating

The secret to making this dish is the heat of the oil and the speed at which the squid is cooked. It should be deep-fried at 350–400°F (180–200°C) for no more than 1 minute; this ensures that the squid will be tender. If cooked for any longer, the squid tends to become rubbery. Note also that the smaller the squid, the more tender they are likely to be.

Pour oil into a frying pan to a depth of 3 inches (7.5 cm). Heat oil to temperature listed above. Slice squid bodies into rings about ¼ inch (6 mm) thick. Dredge rings in flour, dip into egg mixture then coat with breadcrumbs. Fry squid for 1 minute. Drain on paper towels and serve immediately.

Grilled shrimp

Gambas a la plancha

Serves 8

8 cloves garlic, coarsely chopped
1/2 cup (4 fl oz/125 ml) olive oil
2 lb (1 kg) shrimp (prawns), shells intact
chopped parsley, for garnish
Garlic mayonnaise (see page 59), for serving

In a small bowl, marinate garlic in olive oil for at least 30 minutes. Oil a heavy large frying pan and place over medium-high heat. Add as many shrimp as will fit in one layer. Drizzle about 1 teaspoon of olive oil over each shrimp, add some garlic and cook for 2 minutes. Turn shrimp, drizzle with a little more olive oil and cook for 2 more minutes, then remove from heat. Do not overcook or shrimp will become mushy.

Wipe pan with a paper towel and repeat process until all shrimp are cooked. Keep shrimp warm in a low oven while you cook remainder. Sprinkle with chopped parsley and serve with Garlic mayonnaise.

HINTS *A la plancha* simply means that a food is grilled, a very common method of cooking seafood and steaks in Spain. The best way to achieve the same results is to use a large, heavy frying pan that has been lightly oiled, with small amounts of oil added during cooking. The shrimp are cooked a few at a time, so each remains in contact with the bottom of the pan. Alternatively, the shrimp can be cooked on a barbecue and basted with olive oil and garlic.

Garlic shrimp

Gambas al Ajillo

Serves 8

8 cloves garlic, finely chopped
4 red chili peppers, seeded and chopped
olive oil as needed
2 lb (1 kg) shrimp (prawns), peeled and deveined
coarse salt

Divide garlic and chilies among 8 individual, flameproof ramekins. To each ramekin add enough oil to just cover shrimp when added later. Heat over high heat until garlic turns golden brown. Add shrimp and remove from heat after 1 minute. Sprinkle with coarse salt. Serve immediately with plenty of crusty bread.

Stuffed lobster tails

Langosta rellena

Serves 8

8 small lobster tails, about 3 oz (100 g) each
1/4 cup (2 fl oz/60 ml) olive oil
2 onions, finely chopped
4 cloves garlic, finely chopped
1 tablespoon peeled and finely chopped fresh ginger
2 tablespoons chopped fresh cilantro (coriander), plus 2 tablespoons roots, chopped
4 scallions (shallots/spring onions), finely chopped, plus green tops, finely chopped
1/2 cup (4 fl oz/125 ml) cognac
1 tablespoon hot paprika
2 tablespoons Chili sauce (see page 58)
4 red bell peppers (capsicums), roasted, peeled and seeded (see page 12), then pureed
1 cup (8 oz/250 g) whole peeled tomatoes, pureed
2 tablespoons red wine vinegar
2 tablespoons butter

Remove meat from each lobster tail, leaving shell intact. Blanch shells in a saucepan of boiling water for 2–3 minutes. Drain and rinse thoroughly. Remove tough outer skin from lobster meat and cut meat crosswise into slices 1/2–3/4 inch (1–2 cm) thick.

In a saucepan over medium heat, warm oil. Sauté onions, garlic, ginger, cilantro roots and white part of scallions for 4 minutes. Add cognac and cook for 1 minute. Add paprika, Chili sauce, bell pepper puree, tomato puree and vinegar and simmer for 15–20 minutes.

In another frying pan, melt butter and gently sauté lobster slices with green scallion tops and cilantro leaves. When lobster has changed color and is half cooked, drain and add lobster to sauce. Simmer until lobster is opaque throughout (do not overcook). Remove lobster from sauce and arrange in shells. Top with sauce and serve.

Batter-fried fish

Pescado frito

Serves 8

1 cup (8 fl oz/250 ml) cold water

1 cup (4 oz/125 g) all-purpose (plain) flour

1/2 cup (2 oz/60 g) cornstarch (cornflour)

pinch of salt

dash of lemon juice

1 egg yolk

1 lb (500 g) bream, porgy or other lean fish

oil, for frying

flour, for dredging

In a bowl, whisk cold water with flour and cornstarch until completely smooth. When you dip a finger into batter, it should run off, leaving just a thin coating on your finger. Whisk in salt, lemon juice and egg yolk. Cover and refrigerate batter for about 15 minutes.

Cut fish into strips about 2¼ by 1¼ inches (6 cm by 3 cm). Pour 3 inches (7.5 cm) oil in a frying pan and heat to 400°F (200°C) on a deep-frying thermometer. Dredge fish in flour and then coat with batter. Fry until golden brown on both sides. Drain on paper towels and serve immediately.

Mussels in spicy tomato sauce

Mejillones en salsa picante de tomate

Serves 8

- 2 tablespoons olive oil
- 2 onions, finely chopped
- 6 cloves garlic, finely chopped
- 1 tablespoon peeled and finely chopped fresh ginger
- 1 bunch cilantro (coriander), roots and leaves finely chopped and kept separated

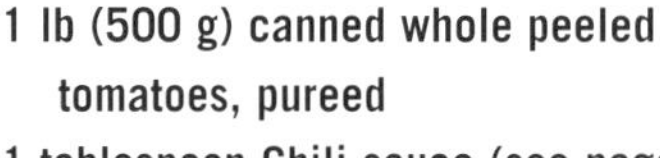

- 1 lb (500 g) canned whole peeled tomatoes, pureed
- 1 tablespoon Chili sauce (see page 58)
- 1¼ cups (10 fl oz/300 ml) dry white wine
- 2 lb (1 kg) mussels, scrubbed and debearded
- cilantro (coriander) sprigs, for garnish
- salt

In a pot large enough to accommodate all ingredients, warm oil over medium heat. Sauté onions, garlic, ginger and cilantro roots in olive oil for 3–4 minutes. Add tomatoes, Chili sauce, wine and salt to taste and simmer for about 10 minutes. Add cilantro leaves and mussels. Increase heat and cover pot. As mussels open, remove them from pot and divide among 8 small bowls, checking cooking pot every 2 minutes (open mussels left in liquid will shrink and toughen). It will take 6–10 minutes for all mussels to open; discard any that do not open after this time.

Pour sauce over mussels. Garnish with cilantro sprigs and serve with warm, crusty bread to soak up the sauce.

Seafood medley

Zarzuela tapa

Serves 10

4 small crabs about 4 oz (125 g) in total or 1 lb (500 g) crabmeat, raw or cooked
2 tablespoons olive oil
1 onion, finely diced
4 cloves garlic, finely chopped
8 jumbo shrimp (king prawns), heads removed, leaving shells intact
8 oz (250 g) tuna or other firm-fleshed fish such as cod,
cut into 3/4-inch (2-cm) cubes
1 cup (8 fl oz/250 ml) fish stock
1 lb (500 g) canned whole peeled plum (Roma) tomatoes
3 red chili peppers, seeded and chopped, or 1 tablespoon Chili sauce (see page 58)
1/4 cup (2 fl oz /60 ml) cognac
1/2 cup (4 fl oz/125 ml) dry white wine
1 tablespoon chopped parsley
32 mussels, scrubbed and debearded
salt

Clean crabs and cut down center so that each half has a claw attached. Set aside.

Heat oil in a large frying pan over medium heat. Sauté onion and garlic for 2 minutes. Add shrimp, crabs (if raw) and fish cubes. Add about half of fish stock and simmer, removing seafood as it is almost cooked. When all seafood is cooked, add remaining fish stock to pan along with tomatoes, chilies, cognac, wine and parsley and simmer for 10 minutes. Add mussels and cook, removing them as they open and discarding any that do not open.

Divide mussels among 8 bowls. Add crab (if cooked), shrimp and fish to simmering sauce and cook for 2 minutes. Divide seafood and sauce among bowls and serve at once.

Spicy marinated sardines

Sardinas en escabeche picante

Serves 15–20

2 lb (1 kg) fresh sardines
olive oil, for frying
flour, seasoned with salt and a little chili powder, for dredging

FOR ESCABECHE

4 cups (32 fl oz/1 L) olive oil
20 cloves garlic, peels intact, crushed
2 large onions, thinly sliced
1 tablespoon peeled and minced fresh ginger
1 tablespoon chopped cilantro (coriander) root
1 cup (8 fl oz/250 ml) tomato puree
2 tablespoons tomato paste
3 cups (24 fl oz/750 ml) red wine vinegar
12 bay leaves
1–2 tablespoons Chili sauce (see page 58)
2 tablespoons chopped cilantro (coriander)
salt
4 red bell peppers (capsicums) roasted, peeled and seeded (see page 12), then cut into strips

Clean sardines and cut off and discard heads. Rinse and dry fish. Pour enough oil in a frying pan to cover bottom generously and place pan over medium heat. Dredge fish in seasoned flour, shaking off excess. Brown quickly on both sides; do not cook through. Drain on paper towels.

To make escabeche: Heat oil in a nonaluminum pot until moderately hot. Add garlic, onions, ginger and cilantro root and cook for 5 minutes. Stir in tomato puree, tomato paste, vinegar, bay leaves, Chili sauce, cilantro and salt to taste, and simmer for 30 minutes. Meanwhile, layer sardines compactly in an earthenware or stainless steel bowl, interspersing layers with red bell pepper strips. Pour marinade over sardines, making sure all are well covered. Let cool, then cover and refrigerate for at least 4 days before serving; during this time, the sardine bones soften completely. Serve chilled.

NOTE This is an adaptation of the traditional Spanish method of preserving sardines. If you prefer the Spanish marinade, omit the ginger, chili sauce and cilantro, and add sprigs of fresh thyme and oregano with the vinegar.

Seafood croquettes

Croquetas de pescado

Serves 12–15

7 tablespoons butter
1 cup (4 oz/125 g) all-purpose (plain) flour
1 cup (8 fl oz/250 ml) milk
1/2 cup (4 fl oz/125 ml) white wine
2 teaspoons hot paprika
salt and freshly ground pepper
10 oz (300 g) boned cod or other white-fleshed fish
3 oz (90 g) shrimp (prawns) peeled, deveined and chopped
1/2 cup (1 oz/30 g) chopped parsley
3 oz (90 g) mussels, cooked and finely chopped
flour, for dredging
2 eggs beaten with a little water
breadcrumbs, for coating
oil, for frying

Melt butter in a frying pan over low heat. Stir in flour and cook, stirring constantly, for 2–3 minutes; make sure the roux doesn't burn. Little by little, whisk in milk and wine. Add paprika and salt and pepper to taste and whisk until mixture is completely smooth. Stir in fish, shrimp and parsley and cook for 5 minutes. Remove from heat and stir in mussels. Let mixture cool, then refrigerate for at least 3–4 hours or, preferably, overnight.

Shape seafood mixture into croquettes about 3 inches (7.5 cm) long and 1 inch (2.5 cm) in diameter. Roll in flour, dip into beaten eggs and then coat with breadcrumbs. For best results, refrigerate for at least 30 minutes.

In a frying pan, heat enough oil to cover croquettes. Oil is ready when a bread cube dropped in hot oil sizzles on contact. Fry croquettes, turning once, until golden brown. Drain on paper towels and serve immediately.

Squid and octopus salad

Ensalada de calamares y pulpo

Serves 8–10

3 lb (1.5 kg) baby octopus, tenderized (see pages 60–61)
3 lb (1.5 kg) squid
1 cup (8 fl oz/250 ml) white wine vinegar
1 onion studded with 12 cloves
6 bay leaves
12 white peppercorns
1 teaspoon salt
1 tablespoon finely chopped fresh dill
1 cup (8 fl oz/250 ml) olive oil
½ cup (4 fl oz/125 ml) freshly squeezed lemon juice
lemon wedges, for serving
freshly ground pepper

Clean octopus, removing and discarding heads. Clean squid thoroughly, discarding heads but retaining tentacles. In a large pot, bring 3–4 quarts (3–4 L) of water to boil. Add vinegar, clove-studded onion, bay leaves, peppercorns and salt; boil for about 10 minutes. Add squid and octopus and cook until tender, about 20–30 minutes. Lift squid and octopus from liquid and refresh under cold running water. Remove any skin from seafood. Discard contents of pot. Cut octopus and squid tentacles into chunks and slice squid bodies into very thin rings.

In a glass or ceramic bowl, mix seafood with dill, olive oil and lemon juice. Cover and marinate overnight in refrigerator. Serve with lemon wedges and pepper.

Oyster platter

Plato variado de ostras

Serves 6

36 oysters in the half shell
3 teaspoons red caviar
3 teaspoons black caviar
1 cup tomato cocktail (below)
1 lime, halved
freshly ground pepper
½ cup (4 fl oz/125 ml) prepared béchamel sauce
½ cup (4 oz/125 g) grated sharp cheddar cheese
3 teaspoons grated Parmesan cheese
1 cup (2 oz/60 g) finely chopped spinach leaves
1 tablespoon diced bacon
3 teaspoons Worcestershire sauce
lemon wedges, for garnish
rock salt

FOR TOMATO COCKTAIL
dash Worcestershire sauce
2 drops tabasco sauce
¼ fl oz (8 ml) lemon juice
salt and pepper, to taste
1 cup (8 fl oz/250 ml) tomato juice

To make tomato cocktail: In a small bowl, mix Worcestershire sauce, tabasco sauce, lemon juice and salt and pepper to taste. Mix until well combined and top with tomato juice.

Arrange 18 oysters on a platter large enough to accommodate them. Place ½ teaspoon of red caviar and ½ teaspoon of black caviar on 6 oysters. Top 6 oysters with tomato cocktail. Squeeze lime juice over last 6 oysters and season with pepper. Place remaining 18 oysters on a broiler (grill) pan. In a saucepan, combine half of béchamel sauce with half of cheddar cheese. Heat gently, stirring occasionally, until cheese is melted and combined with sauce. Spoon cheese mixture over 6 oysters and top with Parmesan cheese.

In a saucepan, blanch spinach in boiling water for 2 minutes. Drain and squeeze dry. In a saucepan combine spinach with remaining béchamel and cheddar cheese. Heat gently, stirring occasionally, until cheese has melted. Spoon spinach mixture over next 6 oysters. Top last 6 oysters with bacon and drops of Worcestershire sauce.

Place pan under broiler (grill) and cook oysters until sauces begin to brown and bubble. Arrange on platter with first 18 oysters. Serve with lemon wedges.

Make Your Own...

The following chili sauces make a delicious addition to tapas recipes. The simple tomato sauce (*salsa de tomate*) and mayonnaise (*salsa mayonesa*) are traditional accompaniments and ingredients found in many Spanish recipes. They make ideal dipping sauces for tapas.

Chili sauce

Makes about 1½ cups (12 fl oz/375 ml)

1 lb (500 g) red chili peppers
2½ cups (20 fl oz/625 ml) water
1 tablespoon white vinegar
1 teaspoon superfine (caster) sugar
2 tablespoons peanut oil
½ cup (4 fl oz/125 ml) boiling water

Remove stems from chili peppers. Remove seeds if you want a less fiery sauce. Place chilies and water in a saucepan over medium heat and bring to a boil. Cover, reduce heat to simmer and cook until chilies are soft, about 15 minutes. Drain. Working in batches, place chilies in a food processor and process until smooth. Add vinegar, sugar, peanut oil and boiling water and process to combine. Pour into sterilized jars, seal and refrigerate for up to 1 month.

Sweet chili sauce

Makes 3 cups (24 fl oz/750 ml)

1 tablespoon Chili sauce (see Chili sauce recipe)
1 tablespoon brown sugar
2 tablespoons granulated sugar
3 cups (24 fl oz/750 ml) white wine vinegar

Combine all ingredients in a nonaluminum saucepan and boil for about 10 minutes. Let cool. The sauce keeps in the refrigerator for up to 3 months.

Mayonnaise

Makes 3 cups (24 fl oz/750 ml)

3 egg yolks
1 tablespoon white wine vinegar
pinch of sugar
salt and freshly ground pepper
2 cups (16 fl oz/500 ml) olive oil
1 teaspoon lemon juice

Combine egg yolks, vinegar, mustard, sugar and salt and pepper to taste in a large bowl and whisk to blend. Whisk in oil, a few drops at a time, gradually increasing to a very slow stream as mixture emulsifies. Mix in lemon juice. Taste and adjust seasonings if necessary.

To make in a food processor, add egg yolks to bowl and process while pouring in oil a little at a time. When mixture begins to emulsify and thicken, alternately add remaining ingredients with olive oil until oil is incorporated. Taste and adjust seasonings if necessary.

If mixture separates (which usually occurs when oil is added too quickly), immediately stop mixing, transfer mixture into a bowl, add 2 more egg yolks and mix in remaining ingredients. Then, very slowly and carefully add separated mixture to new mixture.

VARIATION For garlic mayonnaise, add 2 or more minced garlic cloves to egg yolk mixture.

Simple tomato sauce

Makes 3 cups (24 fl oz/750 ml)

olive oil as needed
1 onion, finely chopped
2 cloves garlic, finely chopped or pressed
1 lb (500 g) canned tomatoes, pureed
2 or 3 bay leaves
salt and freshly ground pepper
aromatic herb such as thyme (optional)

Warm a little olive oil in a frying pan over medium heat. Fry onion and garlic until transparent. Add tomatoes, bay leaves, salt and pepper to taste and herb (if using). Simmer for 30 minutes on low to medium heat.

VARIATION For zesty tomato sauce, add 1 red chili pepper to tomatoes.

Glossary

CHILI PEPPERS Red chilies are frequently used in tapas. They are more often used in their dried form to add tang to a dish rather than to make it spicy-hot. Having given this advice, as you will note, I completely ignore it and tend to be heavy-handed with chili in a number of recipes. This is a personal preference and one that has always seemed to meet the approval of people who sample the dishes. Rather than use dried or fresh chilies, however, I often add their flavor in the form of chili sauce, containing red chilies, salt and vinegar. I find that the best way to keep chili on hand is simply to have a jar of chili sauce in the refrigerator. It keeps almost indefinitely, has a great flavor and is available from Asian markets and many delicatessens.

CHORIZO This Spanish pork sausage often has an orange tint due to the presence of paprika. It has many uses and is often sliced and eaten cold or fried and served with bread. Chorizo and other Spanish sausages are available at Spanish, Portuguese or South American delicatessens.

CLAMS Most tapas recipes use small clams. If you are unable to find them, use a larger variety and reduce the quantities of other ingredients in the recipes. But a word of warning: the larger clams are tougher.

COGNAC This is specified in a number of recipes. If you can find good Spanish brandy, it is the preferred ingredient. You can also use French cognac or brandy. Avoid using cheap brandy, as it can mar the flavor of a dish.

OCTOPUS If you cannot obtain tenderized baby octopus or if you have a ready supply of larger fresh octopus, follow this procedure. Holding octopus firmly, beat or throw it forcefully against a hard surface (such as concrete) about 30 or 40 times. Clean each octopus thoroughly and discard the head. Remove the little hard ball (or "beak") in the center of octopus and cut off the last 3/4 inch (2 cm) of tentacles. Half fill a pot large enough to accommodate octopus with water and bring it to a boil. Immerse octopus in boiling water for 30 seconds, then remove it. Bring water back to the boil and repeat the process 3 more times. Bring water to the boil again and add, for each 2 L water, a peeled onion studded with 6 cloves, 1 bay leaf, 6 white peppercorns and 2 tablespoons vinegar. Add octopus and simmer gently. There is no exact formula as to how long to cook octopus; it will depend on how successful you have been in tenderizing it and on the thickness of the tentacles. After one hour, remove a piece of octopus and bite into it to test for tenderness; repeat this process every 15 minutes or so until octopus is tender. (Cooking can take one hour or as long as three.) Drain cooked octopus and cut tentacles into bite-size cross-sections.

OLIVE OIL Where olive oil is specified, it is important to use Spanish olive oil. It has a distinct flavor essential to many of these recipes.

SQUID Pay a little extra and buy small, fresh squid rather than frozen. You have to clean them yourself, but the reward is an infinitely better flavor. To clean squid, pull head and attached intestines from tubelike body. Remove and discard long, thin cartilage. Cut off wings from body if desired and remove eyes and beak from mouth. With your fingers, pull skin from body. Use body tube and tentacles as directed in recipes after rinsing under cold running water.

SERRANO Serrano and jamón serrano are high-quality hams from the mountain regions of Spain. Proscuitto, an Italian ham, is an adequate substitute.

TOCINO This type of cured pork is similar to bacon, with a subtly different flavor. It is often sold in Mediterranean delicatessens, but, if it is not available, use bacon or pancetta.

TOMATOES When tasty vine-ripened tomatoes are unavailable, use a good-quality canned variety for a superior flavor.

Index

Cover picture: Chorizo and olive empanadas, see page 27
Pictured on page 2: Zucchini omelette, see page 34
Pictured on page 4: Potato salad, see page 19

A LANSDOWNE BOOK

Published by Apple Press in 2002
Sheridan House
4th Floor
112-116a Western Road
Hove
East Sussex BN3 1DD UK

Reprinted 2004

Created and produced by Lansdowne Publishing
Text: Richard Tapper
Photographer: Vicki Liley
Designer: Avril Makula
Editor: Joanne Holliman
Production Manager: Sally Stokes
Project Coordinator: Kate Merrifield

ISBN 1 84092 426 8

Set in Trade Gothic, Journal Text, Gill Sans and Neuropol on QuarkXPress
Printed in Singapore by Kyodo Printing